MOTOCROSS

APEX

BY CIARA O'NEAL

WWW.APEXEDITIONS.COM

Apex is distributed by North Star Editions:
sales@northstareditions.com | 888-417-0195

Produced for Apex by Red Line Editorial.

Photographs ©: Michaela Rihova/CTK/AP Images, cover, 1; Shutterstock Images, 4–5, 6–7, 12, 13, 14, 15, 16–17, 19, 20, 21, 22–23, 24, 26, 27, 29; iStockphoto, 8–9, 18, 25; National Photo Company Collection/Library of Congress, 10–11

Library of Congress Control Number: 2021915731

ISBN
978-1-63738-151-9 (hardcover)
978-1-63738-187-8 (paperback)
978-1-63738-257-8 (ebook pdf)
978-1-63738-223-3 (hosted ebook)

Printed in the United States of America
Mankato, MN
012022

NOTE TO PARENTS AND EDUCATORS

Apex books are designed to build literacy skills in striving readers. Exciting, high-interest content attracts and holds readers' attention. The text is carefully leveled to allow students to achieve success quickly. Additional features, such as bolded glossary words for difficult terms, help build comprehension.

TABLE OF CONTENTS

CHAPTER 1

ON YOUR MARKS...

Motocross racers roll up to the starting gate. They rev their bikes' engines. And they lean forward.

Up to 30 riders can take part in a motocross race.

Then the gate drops. Tires spin. Mud flies. Racers rocket along the **straightaway** and into the first turn.

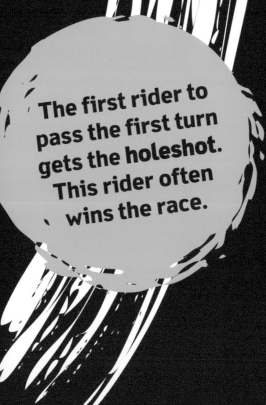

The first rider to pass the first turn gets the holeshot. This rider often wins the race.

Motorcycle riders must lean to turn around corners.

Motocross races have lots of jumps.

Bikes roar toward the first jump. They launch into the air and thud back onto the track. One racer pulls ahead. His bike sails over the finish line. The checkered flag waves. He wins!

ROUGH TRACKS

Motocross tracks test riders' skills. Riders must handle big jumps and fly around tight corners. They often have to ride through slippery mud.

CHAPTER 2

MOTOCROSS HISTORY

The first motorcycle races took place in the early 1900s. British riders raced bikes in timed **motos**. Soon, they went off road. Motocross was born.

A crowd gathers to watch a US motorcycle race in the 1920s.

By the 1950s, motocross had spread across Europe. A group made rules and held official races. Racers did laps around outdoor dirt tracks. Many spectators came to watch.

By the 1960s, motocross had spread as far east as the Soviet Union.

As motocross spread, people raced to build better dirt bikes. This bike came out in 1962.

The word *motocross* combines the French word for motorcycle and the English word *cross-country*.

In the 1960s, the sport reached the United States. And it continued to spread. Today, races are held all over the world.

A rider takes part in the 2013 Motocross World Championship in Thailand.

SUPERCROSS

The first indoor races happened in the 1970s. Riders used dirt tracks in **stadiums**. This new kind of racing became hugely popular. It was called Supercross.

In 1972, the first Supercross championship took place in a stadium in Los Angeles, California.

CHAPTER 3

THE DIRT ON MOTOCROSS

At a motocross event, riders race in two motos. They score points based on how they place in each race. The rider with the most points wins.

Each moto lasts 30 minutes plus two laps.

Jumps are named after the number of hills. A double jump has two hills. A triple has three. A quad has four.

Motocross tracks have **obstacles** such as jumps and bumps. Some tracks also have tunnels. Many have sharp turns, too.

Whoops are rows of small bumps. Rollers have bumps that are larger and rounded.

A rider skips over whoops during a motocross race.

There are many kinds of motocross races. For example, EnduroCross uses long indoor motos. Hillclimbs test how far riders can travel up a steep hill.

EnduroCross races have lots of tough obstacles, such as logs and rocks.

Some freestyle motocross tricks involve letting go of the bike in midair.

FREESTYLE MOTOCROSS

In freestyle events, riders don't race. Instead, they fly off huge jumps. They perform tricks in the air. The best moves win the most points.

CHAPTER 4

READY TO RACE

Motocross racers ride dirt bikes. These motorcycles have metal **frames**. They are strong but light.

A dirt bike's frame is also called a chassis.

The 2019 Kawasaki KX450 is known for its powerful engine.

Dirt bikes have large engines. These powerful engines help riders zoom down the rough track. Knobby tires help grip the dirt.

ENGINE SIZES

Riders **compete** in motos based on their bikes' engine sizes. Bikes with similar engines race together. More advanced riders often use bigger engines. Many races are also divided by age.

Most motocross tracks are between 0.5 and 2 miles (0.8–3 km) long.

The bumps on motocross tires help the bikes dig into the dirt.

Tricky obstacles and hard landings make motocross challenging. The sport can be dangerous, too. Riders wear helmets, **goggles**, and boots for protection.

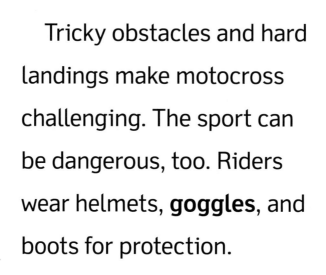

A helmet and goggles are two of the most important pieces of a rider's gear.

Safety gear can keep riders safe even during falls.

Motocross riders wear body armor made from plastic and foam.

COMPREHENSION QUESTIONS

Write your answers on a separate piece of paper.

1. Write a few sentences explaining the main ideas of Chapter 3.

2. Would you like to ride on a motocross track? Why or why not?

3. In which type of motocross event do racers get points by doing tricks?

    A. EnduroCross

    B. hillclimb

    C. freestyle

4. Why do bikes with different engine sizes race in separate groups?

    A. Bikes with different engine sizes can go different speeds.

    B. Bikes with different engine sizes must use different tracks.

    C. Separate groups keep the bikes from crashing.

5. What does **spectators** mean in this book?

Racers did laps around outdoor dirt tracks. Many **spectators** *came to watch.*

    A. people who make rules

    B. people who fix cars

    C. people who watch a sport or event

6. What does **protection** mean in this book?

The sport can be dangerous, too. Riders wear helmets, goggles, and boots for **protection**.

    A. a way to stay safe from danger

    B. a way to take more risks

    C. a way to cause more problems

Answer key on page 32.

GLOSSARY

body armor
Coverings that help keep athletes safe.

compete
To try to beat others in a game or event.

frames
The metal parts that give bikes their shape. A bike's seat, pedals, and wheels attach to the frame.

goggles
Coverings that protect people's eyes. They are often made of rubber or plastic.

holeshot
First past the middle of the first turn of a motocross race.

motos
Races that use motorcycles.

obstacles
Things that block a rider's way.

stadiums
Huge buildings with lots of seating where people can watch sports and other events.

straightaway
The part of a racetrack that is straight.

TO LEARN MORE

BOOKS

Abdo, Kenny. *Motocross*. Minneapolis: Abdo Publishing, 2018.

Hudak, Heather C. *Motocross*. New York: AV2 by Weigl, 2021.

Shaffer, Lindsay. *Motocross Cycles*. Minneapolis: Bellwether Media, 2019.

ONLINE RESOURCES

Visit **www.apexeditions.com** to find links and resources related to this title.

ABOUT THE AUTHOR

Combine humor and a love of picture books. Stir in noisy kids, two cats, and a husband. Add in a pinch of teaching and a dash of being a librarian . . . and voilà! You have author, Ciara O'Neal.

INDEX

B
body armor, 27
boots, 26

D
dirt bikes, 23–24

E
EnduroCross, 20
engines, 5, 24–25
Europe, 12

F
frames, 23
freestyle, 21

G
goggles, 26

H
helmets, 26
hillclimbs, 20
holeshot, 6

J
jumps, 9, 18, 21

M
motos, 11, 17, 20, 25

O
obstacles, 18, 26

R
rollers, 19

S
stadiums, 15
straightaway, 6
Supercross, 15

T
tires, 6, 24

U
United States, 14

W
whoops, 19

Answer Key:
1. Answers will vary; **2.** Answers will vary; **3.** C; **4.** A; **5.** C; **6.** A